SCHOLASTIC

PR1ME™ PROFESSIONAL LEARNING

MATHEMATICAL PROBLEM SOLVING
– THE BAR MODEL METHOD

A professional learning workbook on the key problem solving strategy used by global top performer, Singapore

There are $\frac{2}{7}$ as many apples as pears in a box.
If there are 14 apples, how many pieces of fruit are there altogether?

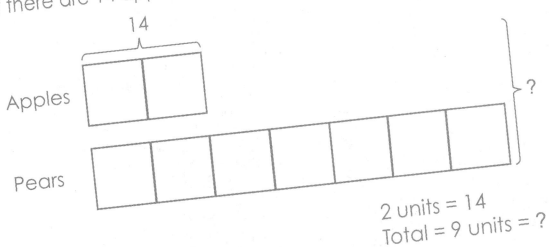

2 units = 14
Total = 9 units = ?

Liu Yueh Mei • Soo Vei Li

For information regarding permission, write to:
Scholastic Education International (Singapore) Pte Ltd
81 Ubi Avenue 4, #02-28 UB.ONE, Singapore 408830
Email: education@scholastic.com.sg

For sales enquiries, write to:

Latin America, Caribbean, Europe (except UK),
Middle East and Africa
Scholastic International
557 Broadway, New York, NY 10012, USA
Email: intlschool@scholastic.com

New Zealand
Scholastic New Zealand Ltd
Private Bag 94407, Botany, Auckland 2163
Email: orders@scholastic.co.nz

Rest of the World
Scholastic Education International (Singapore) Pte Ltd
81 Ubi Avenue 4, #02-28 UB.ONE, Singapore 408830
Email: education@scholastic.com.sg

Visit our website: www.scholastic.com.sg

Australia
Scholastic Australia Pty Ltd
PO Box 579, Gosford, NSW 2250
Email: scholastic_education@scholastic.com.au

United Kingdom
Scholastic Ltd
Euston House, 24 Eversholt Street, London NW1 1DB
Email: education@scholastic.co.uk

India
Scholastic India Pvt. Ltd
A-27, Ground Floor, Bharti Sigma Centre,
Infocity-1, Sector 34, Gurgaon 122001,
Haryana, India
Email: education@scholastic.co.in

First edition 2014
ISBN 978-981-07-8197-2

Printed in the U.S.A. 31
1 2 3 4 5 6 7 8 9 10 25 24 23 22 21 20 19 18 17 16

PREFACE

Professional development of teachers is a critical factor to the success of any classroom environment. The **PR1ME™** Professional Learning series is designed to impart best practices in teaching and empower teachers to achieve excellence in their classrooms.

Mathematical Problem Solving – The Bar Model Method is the first book of this series. It introduces teachers to the fundamentals of using the Bar Model Method (or the Model Method as it is also known), providing the basis and process of understanding different types of word problems and deriving the bar models to solve them.

The Bar Model Method is a key problem solving strategy consistently taught to primary school students in Singapore, a nation acknowledged as a global top performer in mathematics based on its performance in benchmarking studies such as the Trends in International Mathematics and Science Study (TIMSS).

Part 1 of this book provides an overview of the Bar Model Method. It discusses the history of the method and its theoretical underpinnings, its role in the problem solving process and the two basic types of bar models. Part 2 explores the use of the bar model in various topics and is presented in a workbook format. Each chapter in Part 2 brings readers systematically through worked examples that explain how the bar model can be used to solve various types of word problems. This is followed by practice questions which give readers opportunities to apply what they have learned. Learning Points after each section provide the key ideas, while the Reflections section at the end of each chapter encourages readers to consolidate their learning and think about how they can apply it in their classrooms. 'Notes' sections are also provided at the margins and at the end of each chapter in Part 2 for readers to put down their thoughts and ideas.

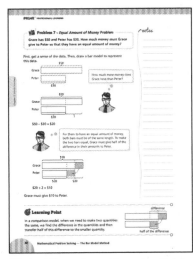

Worked Example and Learning Point

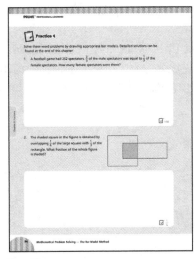

Practice

Reflections

Professional development workshops for teachers are available for this series.
Please contact your local sales representative for more information.

ABOUT THE AUTHORS

Liu Yueh Mei
BSc with Dip in Ed, MEd (NIE/NTU), MA (Stanford University)

An experienced mathematics educator who has served for almost 15 years with the Ministry of Education (MOE), Singapore, as a mathematics curriculum planner and developer as well as Head of Department (Mathematics) in primary schools, Yueh Mei has worked closely with the pioneers and developers of the Singapore Mathematics framework and the Bar Model Method. She is a recipient of the MOE Overseas Postgraduate Scholarship and holds a Master of Arts in Education (MA) with Stanford University and a Master in Education (MEd) with a focus on mathematics problem solving from the National Institute of Education (NIE), a teacher education institute in Nanyang Technological University (NTU), Singapore.

Her current work involves training teachers around the world in Singapore mathematics methodology. She is passionate about promoting the teaching and learning of mathematics through engaged pedagogy to develop conceptual understanding and problem solving. Besides her involvement in training teachers, she also reviews and writes educational materials, provides educational and curricula advice and consultancy to corporations, and serves as an adjunct lecturer at NIE.

Soo Vei Li
BSc (NUS), Dip in Ed (NIE)

Having served for more than 20 years with the Ministry of Education (MOE), Singapore, as a mathematics teacher and Head of Department (Mathematics) in secondary schools, as well as a curriculum planner and developer, Vei Li's work with teachers and schools in Singapore included developing curriculum and teaching strategies to cater to students of wide-ranging abilities. She believes in teaching for conceptual understanding and works closely with teachers on building their pedagogical knowledge in mathematics.

Vei Li is currently a Numeracy Coach at Balaklava High School (South Australia, Australia). Her success in working with Australian teachers on using the Bar Model Method to help students develop fundamental mathematics concepts and proficiencies has inspired her to write this book.

MESSAGE FROM THE AUTHORS

This book is not about short cuts to success in mathematics learning. It is also not about the Bar Model Method as an end-product. It presents an introduction to a visually powerful approach to problem solving involving the concepts of whole numbers, fractions, ratio and percentage to mathematics teachers and educators. In addition to developing problem solving competencies, teachers will see that the appropriate use of this approach will help their students develop multiplicative thinking and proportional reasoning skills. It strives to develop teachers' knowledge and skills in these concepts and, consequently, help their students learn better.

In 2013, at a professional development session for the Literacy and Numeracy National Partnership (LNNP) numeracy coaches in South Australia, Professor Peter Sullivan (Monash University) challenged the group to share as many ways of solving a particular mathematics problem as they could. Amongst the numerous methods presented, Vei Li shared a 'visual' solution which involved drawing a bar model and dividing it into parts. This method has been a major part of the Singapore Primary Mathematics curriculum since the 1980s. The favorable response from the numeracy coaches and interest in this method led us to share this visual method at mathematics conferences in Australia and eventually to writing this book, with the hope that teachers have the opportunity to learn the Bar Model Method and help their students achieve greater success and interest in mathematics.

Both of us had the privilege of working closely with Dr Kho Tek Hong, pioneer of this method, at the Ministry of Education, Singapore, and we saw how his earlier work in the Primary Mathematics Project in the 1980s have resulted in the development of the method and its contribution to the success of mathematics teaching and learning in Singapore. In writing this book, we thank Dr Kho for his guidance and for sharing his insights on mathematics teaching and learning with us, without which this book and our journey would not be possible. In Australia, Vei Li is grateful to her Principal, Mark Healy, and colleagues at Balaklava High School, Professor Peter Sullivan, LNNP Manager, John Bleckly, and fellow numeracy coaches for their encouragement and support.

Liu Yueh Mei
Soo Vei Li

CONTENTS

Part 1
Introducing the
Bar Model Method

Chapter 1

Introduction

I. About the Bar Model Method

The Bar Model Method is a distinctive feature of the Singapore Primary Mathematics Curriculum. It was an innovation in pedagogy that was developed by the Ministry of Education, Singapore, to address a nationwide problem in the 1980s with the purpose of raising mathematical competencies and improving problem solving abilities (Kho, Yeo & Lim, 2009). Since its introduction, it has played an important role in the primary school mathematics curriculum in Singapore.

According to reports quoted in the monograph '*The Singapore Model Method for Learning Mathematics*' published in 2009 by the Ministry of Education, Singapore, a survey in the 1970s conducted prior to the introduction of this method found that 'at least 25% of Primary 6 students did not meet the minimum numeracy level'. In addition to this, a test conducted in 1981 found that primary school students lacked skills in solving word problems with less than 50% of the students being able to solve problems that did not contain key words such as 'altogether' or 'left'.

Against this backdrop, a Primary Mathematics Project (PMP) team was set up and tasked to work on producing instructional materials that would help improve the quality of teaching and learning of mathematics in Singapore. This team, led by Dr Kho Tek Hong, developed the Model Method as a strategy for problem solving.

Following the introduction of this method and Singapore's emphasis on problem solving in its revised curriculum, Singapore made dramatic improvements in its mathematics performance. In international studies such as the Trends in International Mathematics and Science Study (TIMSS), which is conducted every four years at the fourth and eighth grades, students from Singapore consistently performed among the top three in mathematics at both these grades. Table 1 shows Singapore's performance in mathematics across the years at Grade 4. Table 2 shows Singapore's performance at both grades in 2011.

Table 1: Top performing countries across the years (Grade 4)

1995	2003	2007	2011
Singapore	Singapore	Hong Kong	Singapore
South Korea	Hong Kong	Singapore	South Korea
Japan	Japan	Taiwan	Hong Kong
Hong Kong	Taiwan	Japan	Taiwan
Netherlands	Belgium	Kazakhstan	Japan

*No Grade 4 assessment in 1999   Source: http://www.timss.org

Table 2: Top-performing Countries in TIMSS 2011

Fourth Grade	Eighth Grade
Singapore	Korea
Korea	Singapore
Hong Kong SAR	Chinese Taipei
Chinese Taipei	Hong Kong SAR

Source: http://www.timss.org

In 2011, more than 600,000 students from 63 countries and 14 benchmarking entities (regional jurisdictions of countries, such as states) participated in TIMSS.

With the Bar Model Method, students from Singapore learn to solve word problems by drawing either part-whole or comparison models to represent the quantities given in a word problem. The process of solving a word problem using bar models provides students with opportunities to communicate their understanding of the problem using a visual representation. This visual representation gives students a clearer idea of how the known and unknown quantities in the word problem are related, and enhances students' flexibility in manipulating the given data and deciding the operations to use, hence making the understanding of the word problem more accessible. In problems where there is an absence of key words such as 'altogether' and 'left', students use this method as a strategy to guide their approach whilst building their mathematical reasoning capacity.

The Bar Model Method is aligned to the Concrete-Pictorial-Abstract (C-P-A) approach which is the key pedagogical approach adopted in the teaching of mathematics across primary schools in Singapore. It is pictorial in nature and bridges the concrete to the abstract by allowing students to first visualize and understand the problem before progressing to the abstract where numbers, notation and symbols are used.

The method can be taught in the early years of primary school and used consistently as a general problem solving strategy through to middle school years for concepts involving whole numbers, fractions, ratio and percentage. In addition, it brings across and reinforces concepts of multiplicative thinking and proportional reasoning which many struggling learners of mathematics fail to grasp. It also helps to develop pre-algebraic thinking. In the teaching of algebra, teachers are encouraged to build on the Bar Model Method to help students understand and formulate equations when solving algebraic problems.

II. Theoretical Underpinnings of the Bar Model Method

Theoretical underpinnings from Bruner (1961) and Greeno (1978) support the aims and works of the Singapore Mathematics Curriculum.

Pedagogically, the Bar Model Method is aligned to Jerome Bruner's learning theory (Bruner, 1961) consisting of the three modes in representing mathematical ideas — enactive (concrete), iconic (pictorial) and symbolic (abstract). This theory suggests that new concepts be taught first through the use of concrete manipulation (enactive knowledge). This should be followed by pictorial representation (iconic knowledge) which acts as a bridge to the attainment of abstract ideas and formulation (symbolic knowledge).

Cognitive theorists who study the use of schemas, which are building blocks of cognitive processes, also found that within the general semantic categories of addition and subtraction word problems, there is a developmental level where children integrate a 'Part-Part-Whole' schema to represent data and relationship with a slot for an unknown quantity (Nesher, Greeno & Riley, 1982). This 'Part-Part-Whole' schema allows children to manipulate data flexibly and accurately. The Bar Model Method, which is a pictorial representation, much like Greeno's schemas for addition and subtraction word problems, allows students to visualize and make sense of the data and relationships presented in the word problem. It makes visual the 'Part-Part-Whole' schemas and facilitates manipulation of the data visually.

III. The Role of the Bar Model Method in the Problem Solving Process

Problem solving is the central focus in most mathematics curricula around the world today. Solving word problems provides a platform for students to apply mathematical concepts in different situations and plays an important role in developing problem solving skills. The Bar Model Method is one among many strategies that students in Singapore learn to apply in problem solving. This method is a specific variant of the 'Draw a picture' mathematics problem solving strategy shown in Polya's 4-step Problem Solving Process (Polya, 1945) in Step 2 on the next page.

The 4-step Problem Solving Process:

 Understand the problem.

Can you describe the problem in your own words?

What information is given?

What do you need to find?

Is there information that is missing or not needed?

 Plan what to do

What can you do to help you solve the problem?
Here are some things you can do:

- Draw a picture
- Make a list
- Choose an operation
- Guess and check
- Look for a pattern
- Make suppositions

- Act it out
- Work backwards
- Use a before-after scenario
- Restate the problem
- Simplify the problem
- Solve part of the problem

 Work out the Answer

Solve the problem using your plan in Step 2.

If you cannot solve the problem, make another plan.

Show your work clearly.

Write the answer statement.

4 **_Check_**

Read the question again. Did you answer the question?

Does your answer make sense?

Is your answer correct?

You may use the following to help you check your answer:

- Fact families
- Estimation
- Replace the unknown in the problem with your answer.

If your answer is not correct, go back to Step 1.

IV. Types of Bar Models

There are two main types of models used in the Bar Model Method. They are the **part-whole model** and the **comparison model**. Other types of bar models are usually a variation of these two main types.

The Part-Whole Model

Consider this problem:

> Jane has 3 balloons. Ken has 8 balloons. How many balloons do they have altogether?

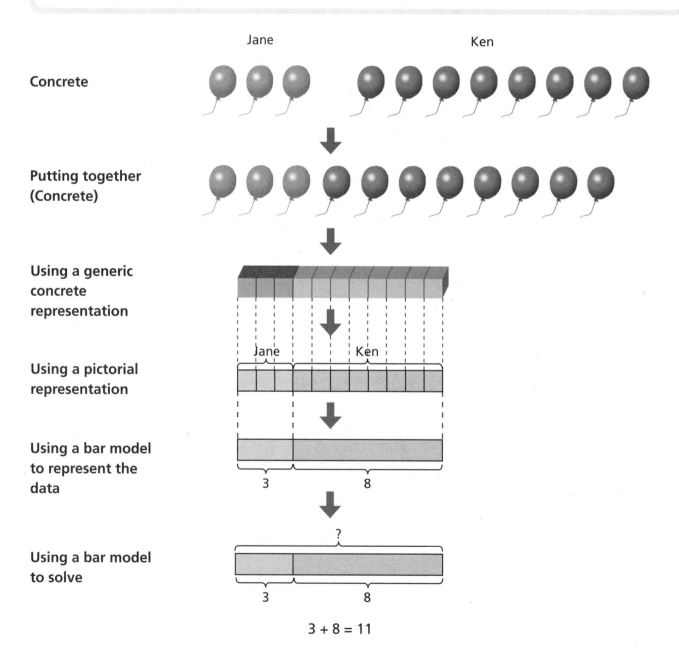

$$3 + 8 = 11$$

They have 11 balloons altogether.

The general representation for the part-whole model is:

whole

part   part

More examples of the part-whole model will be shown in the later chapters.

The Comparison Model

Consider the same scenario with a different question:

> **Jane has 3 balloons. Ken has 8 balloons. How many more balloons does Ken have than Jane?**

For younger students, writing the mathematical sentence '8 – 3 = 5' immediately may be abstract. To help them make sense of the comparison, a one-to-one matching is first shown at the concrete level. The comparison is a parallel to the matching concept.

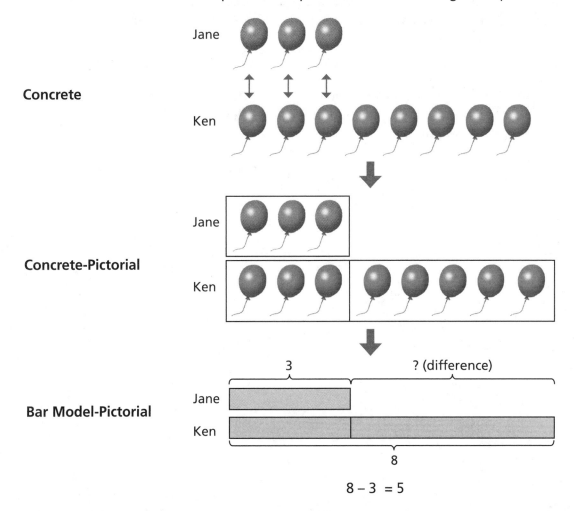

$$8 - 3 = 5$$

Ken has 5 more balloons than Jane.

The comparison model is used to compare two quantities in the problem. It shows the difference between the quantities and reduces students' reliance on equating the terms 'more than' to addition and 'fewer than' to subtraction.

The general representation for the comparison model is:

More examples of the comparison model will be shown in the later chapters.

The part-whole model can be used to illustrate the concept of addition (given the parts, find the whole) and subtraction (given the whole and one part, find the other part). This helps students understand the relationship between quantities and how addition and subtraction are related.

The comparison model, like the part-whole model, illustrates clearly the concept of subtraction when a larger quantity is compared with a smaller quantity. It also illustrates the concept of addition by visually allowing students to see the following:
• smaller quantity + difference = larger quantity
• smaller quantity + larger quantity = total

In the following chapters we will see that these models can also be used to illustrate the concept of the other two operations, multiplication and division. The model presents visually to students the relationship between the number of equal parts, the quantity of each part and the whole.

Part 2
Use of the Bar Model Method in Word Problems

Whole Numbers

In this chapter, we look at word problems involving whole numbers and the four operations, and examine how using the Bar Model Method can help us visualize and solve such problems.

We shall focus on some common types of word problems and their variations. In doing so, we will explore the different types of bar models that can be used to solve these problems effectively.

Word problems involving addition and subtraction

Let us first look at a problem which can be visualized using a part-whole model.

 Problem 1 – *Concert Problem*

147 boys and 95 girls attended a concert. Find the total number of children who attended the concert.

notes

First, get a sense of the data.

Who attended the concert? Were there more boys or more girls?

147 boys and 95 girls attended the concert. So there were more boys.

Next, draw a bar model to represent this data.

Since there are two quantities, boys and girls, I need to draw a bar with two parts. There were more boys. So, I will make the part that represents the number of boys longer.

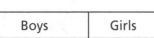

Boys	Girls

Now, transfer the data from the word problem into the model.

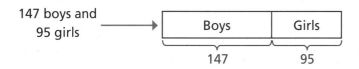

147 boys and 95 girls →

Boys	Girls
147	95

Finally, indicate the unknown.

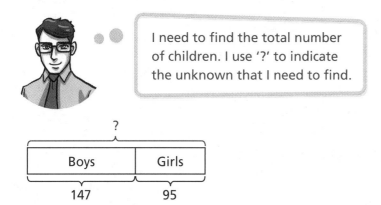

I need to find the total number of children. I use '?' to indicate the unknown that I need to find.

?

Boys	Girls
147	95

From the model, we can see that we need to add 147 and 95 to get the total.

147 + 95 = 242

242 children attended the concert altogether.

Is my answer reasonable?

It is good practice to check your answers after solving each problem. This practice should be instilled in your students as well.

🎯 Learning Point

In Problem 1, two parts are given and we are required to find the whole.

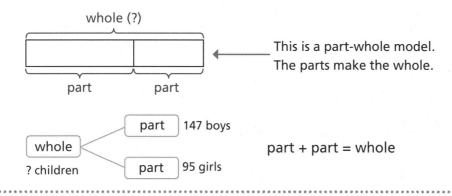

whole (?)

This is a part-whole model.
The parts make the whole.

part   part

whole → part 147 boys
            part 95 girls

? children

part + part = whole

Let us now look at a variation of Problem 1.

242 children attended a concert. If there were 147 boys, how many girls attended the concert?

notes

First, get a sense of the data.

I know the total number of children and the number of boys. I need to find the number of girls.

Then, draw a bar model to represent this data.

I first draw one bar to represent the total number of children or the whole.

Then, I show the two parts, boys and girls, on the bar.

Boys	Girls

Now, transfer the data from the word problem into the model.

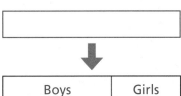

From the bar model, we can see that:

Boys + Girls = Total number of children.

So, we need to subtract 147 (the number of boys) from 242 (the total number of children) to find the number of girls.

242 − 147 = 95

95 girls attended the concert.

Chapter 2: *Whole Numbers*

In this variation to Problem 1, the whole and one part are given and we are required to find the other part.

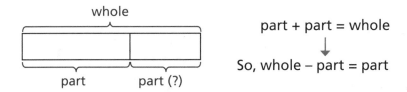

To find one part given the whole and the other part, we subtract the known part from the whole.

Let us look at the variations for Problem 1.

Problem Type	Problem	Solution
Given the parts, find the whole	Parts: 147 and 95; Whole:? ? 147 95	147 + 95 = 242
Given the whole and one part, find the other part	Parts: 147 and ?; Whole: 242 242 147 ? or Parts: 95 and ?; Whole: 242 242 ? 95	242 − 147 = 95 242 − 95 = 147

We have seen how part-whole models are drawn for problems involving two quantities. We can also draw part-whole models for problems involving three or more quantities.

Look at the part-whole model below. It involves three quantities or three parts that make the whole. Can you pose a problem based on this model?

Boys	Girls	Adults
147	95	75

Now, solve the problem that you have posed.

Look at the above part-whole model again. What if the problem posed requires you to compare some of the quantities shown?

The next problem is one such example.

 ### Problem 2 – *Carnival Problem*

There were 147 boys, 95 girls and 75 adults at a carnival. How many more boys than adults were there?

notes

First, get a sense of the data.

In this case, I need to compare two quantities or parts. The quantity for the girls is information that I will not need to use now.

It will be easier to visualize and compare the two parts if I put their bars one above the other. So, I will draw a comparison bar model.

Next, draw a bar model to show the parts that we are comparing.

Boys

Adults

Now, transfer the data from the word problem into the model.

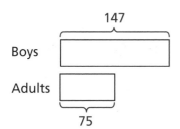

I can now compare the two parts to find out how many more boys than adults there are.

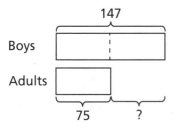

$147 - 75 = 72$

There were 72 more boys than adults.

🎯 Learning Point

In Problem 2, we are required to compare two parts. Putting the bars of the two parts one above the other when comparing allows us to see the difference easily.

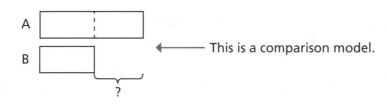

This is a comparison model.

notes

Chapter 2: Whole Numbers

Let us now see how we can make use of the part-whole model and the comparison model to solve other types of word problems involving whole numbers.

 Problem 3 – *Sticker Problem*

Sally has 145 stickers. She has 27 fewer stickers than John. How many stickers do they have altogether?

notes

First, get a sense of the data. Then, draw a bar model to represent this data.

How many people are there?
Who has fewer stickers?
Who has more stickers?

Sally [   ]

John [   ]

There are two people. So, I will draw two bars. John has more stickers. Hence, I will draw a longer bar for John.

Now, transfer the data from the word problem into the model and then solve the problem.

Try this.

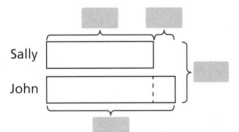

They have _____ stickers altogether.

You can use the process shown above in your classroom as a structure to guide your students in drawing the bar model and then transferring the data into the model.

 Learning Point

When students see the word 'fewer' in a word problem, they tend to subtract the numbers. Drawing a bar model will help students visualize the problem better and correct the misconception that the term 'fewer' always implies that they carry out subtraction. Problem 3 is a good example to show how the model enhances the understanding of why addition rather than subtraction is the correct operation to use in this case.

Practice 1

Solve these word problems by drawing appropriate bar models. Detailed solutions can be found at the end of this chapter.

1. A farmer had 345 apples and oranges. If he had 139 apples, how many oranges did he have?

 206

2. Abel, Bill and Carol have some money. Abel has $20 more than Bill. Bill has $45 less than Carol. Carol has $70. How much do they have altogether?

 $140

Word problems involving multiplication and division

In word problems involving multiplication and division, we often encounter the phrase 'as many as' or 'as much as'. Let us take a look at how we can use bar models to represent and solve such word problems.

 Problem 4 – *Toy Cars Problem*

Henry has 15 toy cars. John has 3 times as many toy cars as Henry. How many toy cars does John have?

First, get a sense of the data. Then, draw a bar model to represent this data.

If John and Henry have the same number of toy cars, the model will look like this.

John [ ]

Henry [ ]

Since John has 3 times as many toy cars as Henry, the model will look like this.

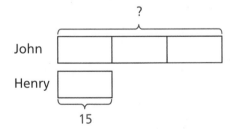

Now, transfer the data from the word problem into the model.

John
Henry
?
15

1 unit ([ ]) represents a certain quantity. In this case, 1 unit represents 15.

Henry has 1 unit. John has 3 units.

  1 unit = 15
  3 units = 15 × 3 = 45

So, John has 45 toy cars.

notes

Let us look at a variation of Problem 4.

John has 3 times as many toy cars as Henry. They have 92 toy cars altogether. How many toy cars does Henry have?

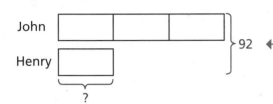

We indicate the total number of toy cars John and Henry have in this way.

4 units = 92
1 unit = 92 ÷ 4 = 23

Since Henry has 1 unit, it means that Henry has 23 toy cars.

Here is another variation of Problem 4.

John has 3 times as many toy cars as Henry. Henry has 42 fewer toy cars than John. How many toy cars do they have altogether?

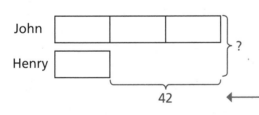

We indicate the difference in the number of toy cars between John and Henry in this way.

2 units = 42
1 unit = 42 ÷ 2 = 21
4 units = 21 × 4 = 84

They have 84 toy cars altogether.

Learning Point

In the variations above, the number of toy cars that Henry or John has is not given. Drawing the comparison model for the two boys allows for better visualization and clarity of the problem. The bar model in each problem allows us to see the number of units each boy has, and either the total or the difference, in quantity and in units. This enables us to understand their relationship and find the unknown easily.

Let us look at the variations for Problem 4.

Problem Type	Problem	Solution
Given the the smaller quantity and an 'as many as' statement showing the relationship between the two quantities, find: (i) the larger quantity (ii) the total quantity	Henry has 15. John has 3 times as many as Henry. John — ? (i) Henry — 15 ? (ii) 1 unit = 15	(i) 1 unit = 15 3 units = 15 × 3 = 45 (ii) 1 unit = 15 4 units = 15 × 4 = 60
Given the bigger quantity and an 'as many as' statement showing the relationship between the two quantities, find: (i) the smaller quantity (ii) the total quantity	John has 3 times as many as Henry. John has 75. 75 John Henry — ? (i) ? (ii) 3 units = 75	(i) 3 units = 75 1 unit = 75 ÷ 3 = 25 (ii) 75 + 25 = 100 or 4 units = 25 × 4 = 100
Given an 'as many as' statement showing the relationship between the two quantities, and the difference between the two quantities, find: (i) the smaller quantity (ii) the larger quantity (iii) the total quantity	John has 3 times as many as Henry. John has 36 more than Henry. ? (ii) John Henry ? (i) 36 ? (iii) 2 units = 36	(i) 2 units = 36 1 unit = 36 ÷ 2 = 18 (ii) 18 × 3 = 54 (iii) 54 + 18 = 72
Given an 'as many as' statement showing the relationship between the two quantities, and the total quantity, find: (i) the smaller quantity (ii) the larger quantity (iii) the difference between the two quantities	John has 3 times as many as Henry. They have 92 altogether. ? (ii) John Henry 92 ? (i) ? (iii) 4 units = 92	(i) 4 units = 92 1 unit = 92 ÷ 4 = 23 (ii) 23 × 3 = 69 (iii) 69 − 23 = 46 or 2 units = 23 × 2 = 46

Practice 2

Solve these word problems by drawing appropriate bar models. Detailed solutions can be found at the end of this chapter.

1. A farmer has 4 times as many chickens as ducks. There are 72 more chickens than ducks. How many chickens and ducks does the farmer have altogether?

 120

2. Emily has 5 times as much money as Luke. If they have $1578 altogether, how much more money does Emily have than Luke?

 $1052

Chapter 2: *Whole Numbers*

3. Nancy, Marcus and Ken shared $364 among themselves. Marcus received 4 times as much money as Ken. Nancy received twice as much money as Marcus. How much money did Marcus receive?

 $112

4. Tara is 6 years younger than her sister, Hannah. 2 years ago, Hannah was 3 times as old as Tara. How old is Tara now?

 5 years old

Problem 5 – *Shared Money Problem*

Mei, Kate and Amy have a total of $159. Mei has $11 more than Kate. Amy has twice as much money as Kate. How much money does Amy have?

First, get a sense of the data. Then, draw a bar model to represent this data.

Should I draw the bars for Mei and Kate, or for Amy and Kate first?

It would be easier representing the 'as many as' or 'as much as' statement first. So, I shall draw the bars for Amy and Kate first.

Amy has twice as much money as Kate. →

Amy

Kate

Next I will add a bar to represent the amount of money Mei has. I can then fill in all the given data into the bar model.

?

Amy

Kate — $11

Mei has $11 more than Kate. The three girls have a total of $159. → Mei

} $159

Chapter 2: *Whole Numbers*

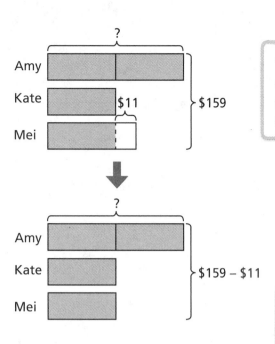

The shaded parts are equal units. If I remove $11 from Mei's bar, then I will have all equal units.

Since I removed $11 from Mei's bar, I also need to remove $11 from the total.

$159 – $11 = $148

4 units = $148
1 unit = $148 ÷ 4 = $37

Amy has 2 units.

2 units = $37 × 2 = $74

So, Amy has $74.

 Problem 6 – *Books Problem*

At a book fair, Rita and Ali bought 32 books altogether. Rita bought 8 more books than Ali. How many books did Ali buy?

First, get a sense of the data. Then, draw a bar model to represent this data.

Since Rita bought more books than Ali, I will draw a longer bar for Rita.

Rita

Ali

Now, transfer the data from the word problem into the model.

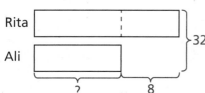

Rita

Ali

⎱32

?   8

Should I divide 32 by 2 first and then subtract 8, or should I subtract 8 first and then divide the new total by 2?

Since Rita and Ali do not have an equal number of books to begin with, I will need to do the latter. So, I will subtract the 8 books first to get all equal units. I then divide the new total by 2.

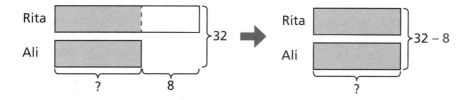

Rita

Ali

⎱32

?   8

Rita

Ali

⎱32 − 8

?

$32 - 8 = 24$

2 units = 24
1 unit = 24 ÷ 2 = 12

Ali bought 12 books.

Learning Point

In Problems 5 and 6, we remove the 'extra' amount from one of the bars to get bars of equal units. We need to subtract this 'extra' amount from the total. Once we have a total that represents equal units, we can divide to get the value that each unit represents.

extra   ⎱total

⎱total − extra

Practice 3

Solve these word problems by drawing appropriate bar models. Detailed solutions can be found at the end of this chapter.

1. A sandwich and a cup of coffee cost $11. The coffee is $3 cheaper than the sandwich. How much is the sandwich?

 $7

2. Ryan and Sarah have a total of 140 picture cards. Sarah and John have a total of 260 picture cards. Given that John has 5 times as many picture cards as Ryan, how many picture cards does Ryan have?

30

3. The cost of 3 shirts and 2 bags is $155. Each bag costs $10 more than each shirt. How much does each shirt cost?

✓ $27

4. Gloria bought 2 pens, a book and a bag from a bookstore. The book cost 3 times as much as the pen and the bag cost $15 more than the book. She spent $175 altogether. What was the cost of the book?

✓ $60

Problem 7 – *Equal Amount of Money Problem*

Grace has $50 and Peter has $30. How much money must Grace give to Peter so that they have an equal amount of money?

First, get a sense of the data. Then, draw a bar model to represent this data.

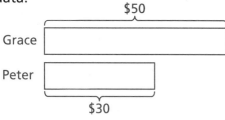

> How much more money does Grace have than Peter?

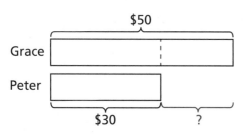

$50 – $30 = $20

> For them to have an equal amount of money, both bars must be of the same length. To make the two bars equal, Grace must give half of the difference in their amounts to Peter.

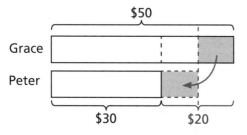

$20 ÷ 2 = $10

Grace must give $10 to Peter.

 Learning Point

In a comparison model, when we need to make two quantities the same, we find the difference in the quantities and then transfer half of this difference to the smaller quantity.

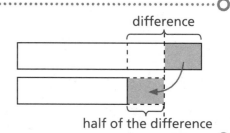

Problem 8 – *Sweets and Chocolates Problem*

There were 3 times as many sweets as chocolates in a jar. After 10 sweets were eaten and another 6 chocolates were added to the jar, there was an equal number of sweets and chocolates in the jar. How many sweets were there in the jar at first?

First, get a sense of the data. Then, draw a bar model to represent this data.

 The number of sweets and chocolates in the jar undergo a change. I can draw 'before and after' bar models to show the quantities at the different times.

Before:

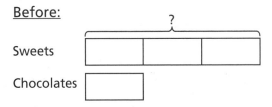

After:

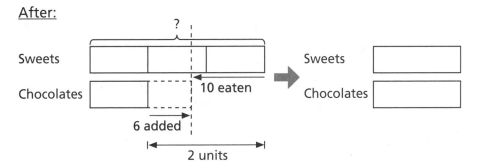

From the bar model above, we can see that:

2 units = 10 + 6 = 16
1 unit = 16 ÷ 2 = 8
3 units = 8 × 3 = 24

There were 24 sweets in the jar at first.

 Learning Point

The question in Problem 8 involves a 'before and after' situation. Drawing two separate bar models, one for 'before' and one for 'after', allows students to visualize the situation pictorially and enables them to then use the given data to solve the problem easily.

Practice 4

Solve these word problems by drawing appropriate bar models. Detailed solutions can be found at the end of this chapter.

1. There were 8 more students in Room A than in Room B. After some students moved from Room A to Room B, both rooms had 32 students each. How many students were there in Room B at first?

 28

2. Mel had 40 more stickers than Jay. After Jay gave away 20 stickers, Mel had 4 times as many stickers as Jay. How many stickers did Mel have at first?

80

Chapter 2: Whole Numbers

Problem 9 – *Spending Money Problem*

At first, Matthew had $142 and Mark had $37. After they each spent an equal amount of money, Matthew had 4 times as much money as Mark. How much did each of them spend?

First, get a sense of the data. Then, draw a bar model to represent this data.

The boys had different amounts of money at different times. I can draw 'before and after' bar models to help me solve the problem.

Before:

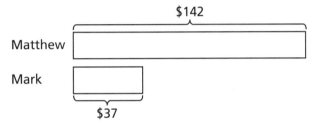

After:

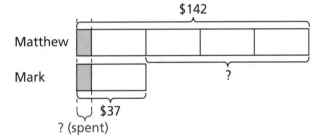

$142 – $37 = $105
3 units = $105
1 unit = $105 ÷ 3 = $35
$37 – $35 = $2

Each of them spent $2.

 Learning Point

In most cases when we need to adjust quantities, we usually do so from the end of the bars. Problem 9 shows us that in this case where an equal quantity is to be removed from both bars, we can remove it from the beginning of the bars. Removing the quantity from the end in this case will not visually simplify the problem and allow us to equate a certain number of units to a quantity.

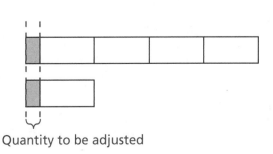

Quantity to be adjusted

Practice 5

Solve these word problems by drawing appropriate bar models. Detailed solutions can be found at the end of this chapter.

1. Shelf A had 40 books and Shelf B had 16 books. After Siti borrowed an equal number of books from Shelf A and Shelf B, there were 3 times as many books on Shelf A than on Shelf B. How many books did Siti borrow altogether?

 8

2. Gayle and Jerry had some money. After their mother gave each of them $20, Gayle had twice as much money as Jerry and Jerry had $50 less than Gayle. How much money did Gayle have at first?

 $80

🔍 Reflections

- There are two main types of bar models — the part-whole model and the comparison model. For any given problem, consider whether a part-whole or a comparison model is more suitable.

- Transfer the data from the word problem into the model, and indicate the unknown(s) with a '?'.

- Study the bar model and information to decide what operations to use to solve the problem.

- In a multiplication and/or division problem, manipulate and equate the quantities to the number of units. This helps reinforce multiplicative thinking and develops pre-algebraic thinking.

How can you apply what you have learned in this chapter to help your students improve their problem solving skills?

Try This...

- Create a word problem involving whole numbers that your students generally have difficulties with.

- Use the Bar Model Method to solve the problem you created. Highlight the critical teaching points in the solution.

Solutions

Page 16:

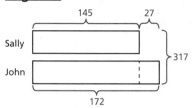

Practice 1

1.

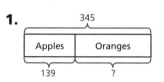

345 – 139 = 206

He had 206 oranges.

2.

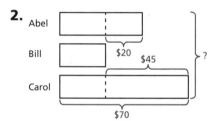

Bill: $70 – $45 = $25
Abel: $25 + 20 = $45
Altogether: $45 + $25 + $70 = $140

or

Bill: $70 – $45 = $25
Altogether: ($25 × 2) + 20 + $70 = $140

They have $140 altogether.

Practice 2

1.

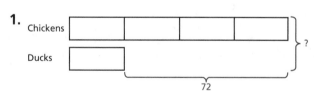

3 units = 72
1 unit = 72 ÷ 3 = 24
5 units = 24 × 5 = 120

The farmer has 120 chickens and ducks altogether.

2.

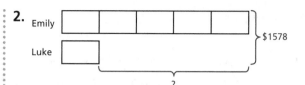

6 units = $1578
1 unit = $1578 ÷ 6 = $263
4 units = $263 × 4 = $1052

or

$1578 – $263 = $1052

Emily has $1052 more than Luke.

3.

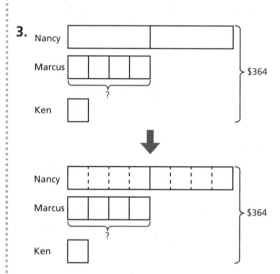

13 units = $364
1 unit = $364 ÷ 13 = $28
4 units = $28 × 4 = $112

Marcus received $112.

4. 2 years ago:

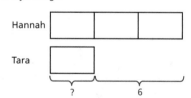

2 units = 6 years old
1 unit = 6 ÷ 2 = 3 years old

2 years ago, Tara was 3 years old.
3 + 2 = 5

Tara is now 5 years old.

Practice 3

1.

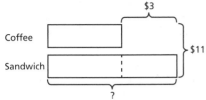

$11 + $3 = $14
$14 ÷ 2 = $7
or
$11 − $3 = $8
$8 ÷ 2 = $4
$4 + $3 = $7

The sandwich costs $7.

2. John has 5 times as many picture cards as Ryan.

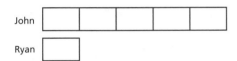

Ryan and Sarah have a total of 140 picture cards.

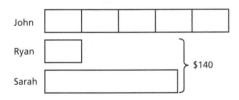

Sarah and John have a total of 260 picture cards.

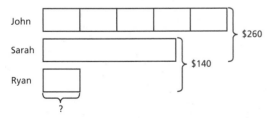

John (5 units) + Sarah = 260
Ryan (1 unit) + Sarah = 140
So, 4 units = 260 − 140 = 120
1 unit = 120 ÷ 4 = 30

Ryan has 30 picture cards.

3.

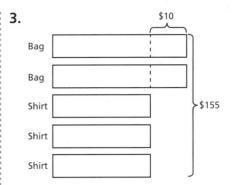

$155 − $20 = $135
$135 ÷ 5 = $27

Each shirt costs $27.

4.

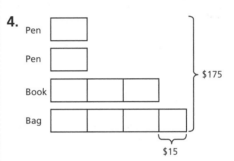

$175 − $15 = $160
8 units = $160
1 unit = $160 ÷ 8 = $20
3 units = 3 × $20 = $60

The cost of the book was $60.

Practice 4

1. Before:

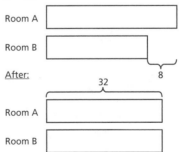

For Room A and Room B to have an equal number of students, half of the extra students in Room A must move to Room B.

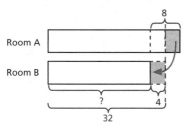

$8 \div 2 = 4$

$32 - 4 = 28$

There were 28 students in Room B at first.

2. Before:

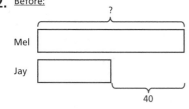

After:

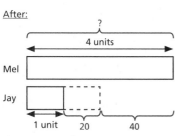

$3 \text{ units} = 40 + 20 = 60$

$1 \text{ unit} = 60 \div 3 = 20$

$4 \text{ units} = 20 \times 4 = 80$

Mel had 80 stickers at first.

Practice 5

1. Before:

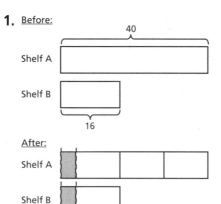

$40 - 16 = 24$

$2 \text{ units} = 24$

$1 \text{ unit} = 24 \div 2 = 12$

$16 - 12 = 4$

$4 + 4 = 8$

Siti borrowed 8 books altogether.

2. Before:

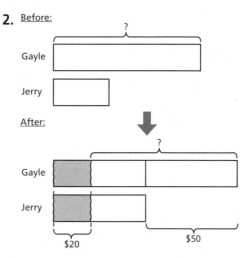

$1 \text{ unit} = \$50$

$2 \text{ units} = \$50 \times 2 = \$100$

$\$100 - \$20 = \$80$

Gayle had \$80 at first.

Chapter 2: *Whole Numbers*

✏notes

Fractions

Word problems involving the part-whole model

As teachers, we often ask students questions similar to the one shown below when we teach the topic on fractions.

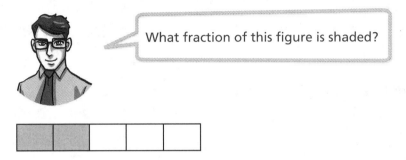

What fraction of this figure is shaded?

Most students would be able to respond correctly. In this case, it would be:

'$\frac{2}{5}$ of the figure is shaded.'

The figure above is a good starting point to introducing and understanding the use of a part-whole model in word problems involving fractions. It is an example of how a part-whole model for fractions can be represented.

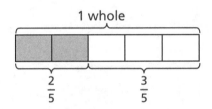

Parts: 2 units and 3 units
Whole: 5 units

The fraction $\frac{2}{5}$ simply means 2 units out of 5 units. The whole represents the total value, where the total value can be any number. For example, if the whole is 20, we can find the quantity represented by $\frac{2}{5}$ of the whole in this way:

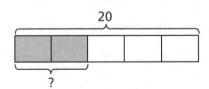

5 units = 20
1 unit = 20 ÷ 5 = 4
2 units = 4 × 2 = 8

So, $\frac{2}{5}$ of the whole is 8.

Let us now look at how we can use the part-whole model to solve word problems involving fractions where the whole is given.

Problem 1 – *Classroom Problem*

There are 30 students in a class. $\frac{3}{5}$ of the students in the class are girls and the rest are boys. How many boys are there?

First, get a sense of the data. Then, draw a bar model to represent this data.

I know the total number of students. I first draw a bar to represent the number of students or the whole.

The fraction given in the word problem is $\frac{3}{5}$. I show $\frac{3}{5}$ on the model by dividing the bar into 5 equal units and shading 3 out of the 5 units.

Now, transfer the data from the word problem into the model.

The whole quantity of 30 students is represented by 5 units.

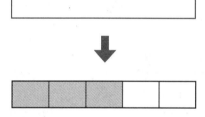

3 units represent the number of girls.
So, 2 units represent the number of boys.

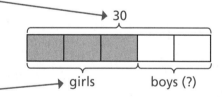

girls   boys (?)

5 units = 30
1 unit = 30 ÷ 5 = 6
2 units = 6 × 2 = 12

There are 12 boys.

Chapter 3: Fractions

notes

Let us now look at a variation of Problem **1.**

$\frac{3}{5}$ of the students in a class are girls. The rest are boys. There are 10 boys. How many girls are there?

First, get a sense of the data.

In this question, the quantity for a part is given.

Then, draw a bar model to represent this data.

Since the denominator of the given fraction is 5, it means that the class is divided into fifths. I draw a bar model with 5 units to represent the total number of students in the class.

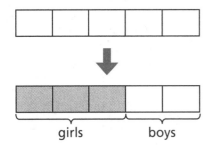

girls   boys

Next, I indicate the parts that represent the girls and the boys.

Girls: $\frac{3}{5}$ (3 units)

Boys: Remaining units (2 units)

Now, transfer the data from the word problem into the model.

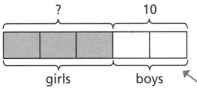

?   10

girls   boys

2 units represent the 10 boys.

2 units = 10
1 unit = 10 ÷ 2 = 5
3 units = 5 × 3 = 15

There are 15 girls.

Learning Point

In Problem 1, the quantity for the whole was given. Hence, by multiplying the fractional part $\left(\frac{3}{5}\right)$ by the whole (30), we can obtain the quantity for the part. In the variation to Problem 1, students tend to similarly perform $\frac{3}{5} \times 10$ to get the answer. This is a common mistake students make when they do not understand the relationship between the quantities given. As 10 is not the quantity for the whole, it is incorrect to perform $\frac{3}{5} \times 10$. Drawing a bar model will help students relate the quantity 10 visually to the number of units representing the boys, hence helping them solve the problem correctly.

Let us look at the variations for Problem 1.

Problem Type	Problem	Solution
Given the quantity for the whole, find a part	There are 240 students. $\frac{1}{4}$ are girls. The rest are boys. 240 (i) ? (girls)　(ii) ? (boys)　　4 units = 240	(i) 4 units = 240 　1 unit = 240 ÷ 4 = 60 (ii) 3 units = 60 × 3 = 180
Given the quantity for a part, find the other part or the whole	$\frac{1}{4}$ of a class are girls. The rest are boys. There are 7 girls. (ii) ? (whole) 7 (girls)　(i) ? (boys)　　1 unit = 7	(i) 1 unit = 7 　3 units = 7 × 3 = 21 (ii) 4 units = 7 × 4 = 28
Given the quantity for the derived part, find the other part or the whole	$\frac{1}{4}$ of a class are girls. The rest are boys. There are 24 boys. (ii) ? (whole) (i) ? (girls)　24 (boys)　　3 units = 24	(i) 3 units = 24 　1 unit = 24 ÷ 3 = 8 (ii) 4 units = 8 × 4 = 32
Given the quantity for the difference, find the parts or the whole	$\frac{1}{4}$ of a class are girls. The rest are boys. There are 16 more boys than girls. (iii) ? (whole) (i) ? (girls)　(ii) ? (boys)　　2 units = 16	(i) 2 units = 16 　1 unit = 16 ÷ 2 = 8 (ii) 3 units = 8 × 3 = 24 (iii) 4 units = 8 × 4 = 32

Note: The key strategy in all the above variations is to equate the given quantity to its corresponding units.

Chapter 3: Fractions

Practice 1

Solve these word problems by drawing appropriate bar models. Detailed solutions can be found at the end of this chapter.

1. Amy had \$240. $\frac{1}{6}$ of her money was spent on a dress. $\frac{1}{2}$ of her money was spent on a pair of shoes. How much money was left?

 \$80

2. Some children were at a school camp. $\frac{5}{8}$ of them were girls. If there were 40 girls at the school camp,

   (a) how many boys were there at the school camp?

   (b) how many more girls than boys were there?

(a) 24 (b) 16

3. Sam read $\frac{4}{7}$ of a book on Friday. He has 42 more pages to read before he will reach the end of the book. How many pages did he read on Friday?

 56

4. A jar was full of 50¢ and $1 coins. $\frac{2}{5}$ of the coins in the jar were 50¢ coins. The rest were $1 coins. There were 10 more $1 coins than 50¢ coins. How many coins were there in the jar altogether?

✓ 50

Word problems involving the comparison model

In the previous chapter, we used the comparison model when comparing two or more quantities. The same applies to fractions.

Look at this model.

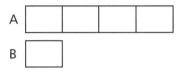

I can say that A is 4 times as much as B, or A is 4 times of B.

I can also say that B is $\frac{1}{4}$ as much as A, or B is $\frac{1}{4}$ of A.

When we say that A is 4 times of B, B is the base to which A is being compared.

When we say that B is $\frac{1}{4}$ of A, A is the base to which B is being compared.

Let us look at a few more examples of comparison models and the relationship between the two quantities in such models.

Model 1:

A is 3 times of B.	⟶ B is the base.
B is $\frac{1}{3}$ of A.	⟶ A is the base.
A is $\frac{3}{4}$ of (A and B).	⟶ Total of A and B is the base.
B is $\frac{1}{4}$ of (A and B).	

Model 2:

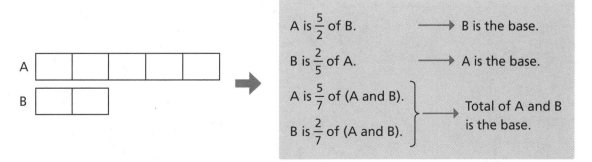

A is $\frac{5}{2}$ of B.	⟶ B is the base.
B is $\frac{2}{5}$ of A.	⟶ A is the base.
A is $\frac{5}{7}$ of (A and B).	⟶ Total of A and B is the base.
B is $\frac{2}{7}$ of (A and B).	

Now, fill in the missing information based on the bar model shown.

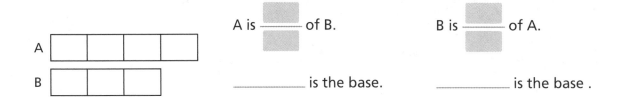

A

B

A is ──── of B.

_____ is the base.

B is ──── of A.

_____ is the base .

Let us now see how we can draw the comparison model to solve word problems involving fractions.

 Problem 2 – *Apples and Pears Problem*

There are $\frac{2}{7}$ as many apples as pears in a box. If there are 14 apples, how many pieces of fruit are there altogether?

notes

First, get a sense of the data. Then, draw a bar model to represent this data.

$\frac{2}{7}$ as many apples as pears

↓

2 units of apples and 7 units of pears

I can also see this relationship using ratio:

apples : pears = 2 : 7

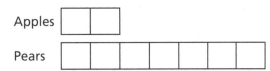

Apples

Pears

Now, transfer the data from the word problem into the model.

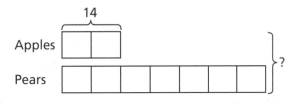

14

Apples

Pears

?

2 units = 14
1 unit = 14 ÷ 2 = 7
9 units = 7 × 9 = 63

There are 63 pieces of fruit altogether.

Learning Point

In Problem 2, the statement 'There are $\frac{2}{7}$ as many apples as pears in a box.' uses a fraction to express how one quantity is proportional to the other. Understanding the relationship between this fraction and the number of units representing each type of fruit is key to drawing the correct bar model.

 Practice 2

Solve these word problems by drawing appropriate bar models. Detailed solutions can be found at the end of this chapter.

1. There are $\frac{3}{7}$ as many pens as pencils in a drawer. If there are 140 pens and pencils altogether, how many pens are there?

 42

2. There are $\frac{2}{5}$ as many bowls as plates in a box. If there are 30 more plates than bowls, how many plates and bowls are there altogether?

70

Problem 3 – *Shopping Problem*

June had $120. She spent $\frac{1}{4}$ of her money on a blouse and $\frac{2}{3}$ of the remainder on a handbag. How much money did she have left?

First, get a sense of the data. Then, draw a bar model to represent this data.

First, I draw a whole to represent the total amount of money June had.

$120

She spent $\frac{1}{4}$ of her money on a blouse.

$120

blouse

She spent $\frac{2}{3}$ of the remaining amount on a handbag.

$120

blouse   remainder

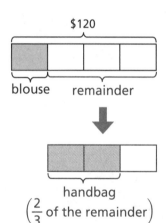

handbag
$\left(\frac{2}{3} \text{ of the remainder}\right)$

$120

blouse handbag amount left

The amount left is represented by 1 unit.

4 units = $120
1 unit = $120 ÷ 4 = $30

June had $30 left.

Solving this word problem without drawing bar models would involve numerous calculations as shown in the two methods below.

Method 1:

$$\frac{1}{4} \times \$120 = \$30$$

She spent $30 on the blouse.

$$\$120 - \$30 = \$90$$

$$\frac{2}{3} \times \$90 = \$60$$

She spent $60 on the handbag.

$$\$120 - \$30 - \$60 = \$30$$

She had $30 left.

or

Method 2:

$$1 - \frac{1}{4} = \frac{3}{4}$$

$$\frac{2}{3} \times \frac{3}{4} = \frac{1}{2}$$

She spent $\frac{1}{2}$ of her money on the handbag.

$$\frac{1}{2} + \frac{1}{4} = \frac{3}{4}$$

$$1 - \frac{3}{4} = \frac{1}{4}$$

She had $\frac{1}{4}$ of her money left.

$$\frac{1}{4} \times \$120 = \$30$$

She had $30 left.

The bar model greatly simplifies the solution to the problem, making such problems accessible to more students including those who have difficulties performing the four operation algorithms on fractions.

 Learning Point

When solving problems involving fractions, it is important to relate the given fraction to the correct 'whole'. This is especially so in problems involving remainders. In Problem 3, the remainder is the new whole for the fraction $\frac{2}{3}$. A bar model makes it visually clear to the students what the fraction of the remainder looks like in relation to the original whole.

Problem 4 – *Pocket Money Problem*

Johan was given some pocket money. He spent $\frac{1}{3}$ of the money

on some game cards and $\frac{1}{4}$ of the remainder on a pen.

What fraction of the money did he have left?

First, get a sense of the data. Then, draw a bar model to represent
this data.

He spent $\frac{1}{3}$ of the pocket
money on game cards.

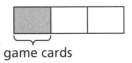

game cards

He then spent $\frac{1}{4}$ of the remainder on a
pen. I need to shade 1 out of 4 units in
the remainder. However there are only
2 units in the remainder!

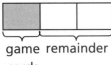

game   remainder
cards

So, I divide each unit further
by 2 to get 4 smaller units in
the remainder.

game   remainder
cards

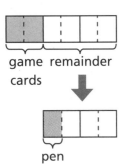

pen

 *notes*

I now have the following:

game pen amount
cards left = $\frac{3}{6}$

$\frac{3}{6} = \frac{1}{2}$

He had $\frac{1}{2}$ the amount of money left.

 Learning Point

The bar model is versatile for manipulation and effective in making relationships visible. In Problem 4, sub-dividing the remainder (2 units into 4 units) is necessary in order to represent '$\frac{1}{4}$ of the remainder'. When we do this, we must also sub-divide the rest of the units in the model so that all the units are equal. This sub-division also reinforces the concept of equivalent fractions as it allows students to see that $\frac{2}{3} = \frac{4}{6}$.

 Practice 3

Solve these word problems by drawing appropriate bar models. Detailed solutions can be found at the end of this chapter.

1. Alan bought some muffins for a party. $\frac{1}{6}$ of the muffins were banana muffins and $\frac{7}{10}$ of the remainder were chocolate muffins. The rest were blueberry muffins. If Alan bought 9 blueberry muffins, how many muffins did he buy altogether?

 36

2. Maria gave some money to each of her three children. Alice received $\frac{1}{5}$ of the money. Kent received $\frac{3}{8}$ of the remainder and Jack received the rest. If Jack received $10, how much did Alice receive?

 $4

3. Rachel read $\frac{1}{3}$ of a book on Monday. She read $\frac{5}{6}$ of the remaining pages on Tuesday and the rest of the book on Wednesday. She read 32 more pages on Tuesday than on Wednesday. How many pages does the book have altogether?

72 pages

Problem 5 – *Age Problem*

$\frac{1}{3}$ of Wayne's age is equal to $\frac{2}{5}$ of Kumar's age. Wayne is 8 years older than Kumar. How old is Wayne?

First, get a sense of the data. Then, draw a bar model to represent this data.

I know that 1 unit of Wayne's age = 2 units of Kumar's age. So, the bar model will look like this.

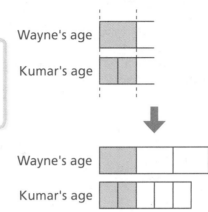

Now, transfer the data from the word problem into the model.

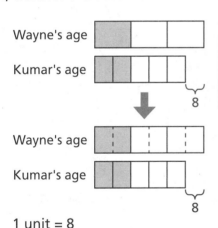

I can divide each unit in Wayne's bar into two smaller units to make both Wayne's and Kumar's units equal.

1 unit = 8
6 units = 8 × 6 = 48

Wayne is 48 years old.

 Learning Point

In Problem 5, each of the fractions given is a fraction of a different whole. It is difficult to see the relationship clearly without drawing a bar model. Drawing a bar model for this problem makes it easy for students to see what 'Fraction of *x* = Fraction of *y*' looks like, where *x* and *y* are two different wholes.

Practice 4

Solve these word problems by drawing appropriate bar models. Detailed solutions can be found at the end of this chapter.

1. A football game had 252 spectators. $\frac{2}{3}$ of the male spectators was equal to $\frac{1}{3}$ of the female spectators. How many female spectators were there?

 168

2. The shaded part in the figure is obtained by overlapping $\frac{1}{4}$ of the square with $\frac{1}{3}$ of the rectangle. What fraction of the whole figure is shaded?

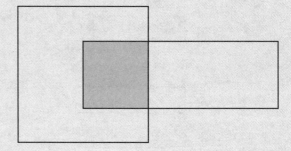

$\checkmark$ $\frac{1}{6}$

Chapter 3: Fractions (side text)

Reflections

Some examples of problems involving fractions that bar models can be used to represent are:

- Problems involving a fraction of a whole, e.g. $\frac{1}{3}$ of 15

- Problems involving a fraction of a remainder, e.g. $\frac{1}{3}$ of the remainder

- Problems involving a fraction that expresses how one quantity is proportional to another quantity, e.g. $\frac{2}{7}$ as many apples as pears

- Problems involving fractions of two different wholes, e.g. fraction of x and fraction of y.

How can you apply what you have learned in this chapter to help your students, including those who have difficulties performing fractions algorithms, develop a better understanding of fractions and solve problems involving fractions?

Try This...

- Create a word problem involving fractions that your students generally have difficulties with.
- Use the Bar Model Method to solve the problem you created. Highlight the critical teaching points in the solution.

Solutions

Page 46:

A is $\frac{4}{3}$ of B.

B is the base.

B is $\frac{3}{4}$ of A.

A is the base.

Practice 1

1.

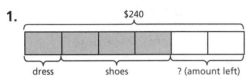

6 units = $240
1 unit = $240 ÷ 6 = $40
2 units = $40 × 2 = $80

$80 was left.

2.

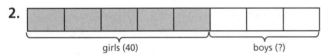

(a) 5 units = 40
1 unit = 40 ÷ 5 = 8
3 units = 8 × 3 = 24

There were 24 boys at the school camp.

(b) 5 units of girls, 3 units of boys
There were 2 more units of girls than boys.
2 units = 8 × 2 = 16

There were 16 more girls than boys.

3.

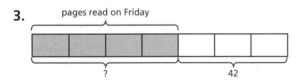

3 units = 42
1 unit = 42 ÷ 3 = 14
4 units = 14 × 4 = 56

He read 56 pages on Friday.

4.

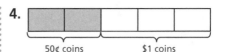

There was 1 more unit of $1 coins than 50¢ coins.
1 unit = 10
5 units = 10 × 5 = 50

There were 50 coins in the jar altogether.

Practice 2

1.

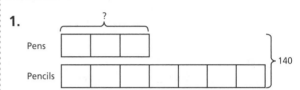

10 units = 140
1 unit = 140 ÷ 10 = 14
3 units = 14 × 3 = 42

There are 42 pens.

2.

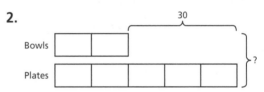

3 units = 30
1 unit = 30 ÷ 3 = 10
7 units = 10 × 7 = 70

There are 70 dishes altogether.

Practice 3

1.

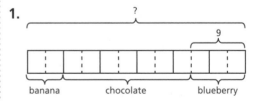

3 units = 9
1 unit = 9 ÷ 3 = 3
12 units = 3 × 12 = 36

Alan bought 36 muffins.

2.

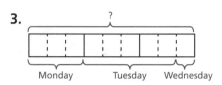

5 units = $10
1 unit = $10 ÷ 5 = $2
2 units = $2 × 2 = $4

Alice received $4.

3.

5 units − 1 unit = 4 units
4 units = 32 pages
1 unit = 32 ÷ 4 = 8 pages
Whole book → 9 units = 8 × 9
= 72 pages

The book has 72 pages altogether.

Practice 4

1.

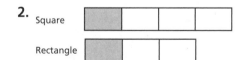

9 units = 252
1 unit = 252 ÷ 9 = 28
6 units = 28 × 6 = 168

There were 168 female spectators.

2.

Total = 6 units (The 2 shaded units overlap to become 1 unit)
Shaded part = 1 unit

$\frac{1}{6}$ of the whole figure is shaded.

✏ *notes*

Ratio

Word problems involving the comparison model

We can use ratios to represent relationships between two or more quantities.

For example, when the ratio of the number of books to the number of magazines is 2 : 3, it means that there are 2 units of books and 3 units of magazines, where each unit represents a quantity.

Using a bar model, the ratio of the number of books to the number of magazines looks like this:

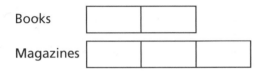

We can assign a quantity to each unit. For example, if each unit represents 5, then we have the following:

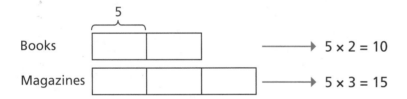

Hence, there are 10 books and 15 magazines.

We can also express the relationship of the books and magazines in the problem above using fractions instead of ratios.

By looking at the bar model above, I can say that the number of books is $\frac{2}{3}$ the number of magazines. I can also say that the number of books is $\frac{2}{5}$ of the total number of books and magazines.

Fractions and ratios can be used interchangeably if we understand their concepts well and how they are represented using bar models.

Let us look at some word problems involving ratio where quantities are given for the parts, the whole or the difference.

 Problem 1 – *Cereal Bar Problem*

In a cereal bar, the ratio of fiber to protein is 5 : 6. If the bar contains 30 grams of fiber, how much protein does it contain?

First, get a sense of the data. Then, draw a bar model to represent this data.

> I can represent the ratio 5 : 6 using a bar model.

Fiber ▭▭▭▭▭

Protein ▭▭▭▭▭▭

Now, transfer the data from the word problem into the model.

> In this problem, the quantity for one part of the ratio is given.
>
> Fiber: 30 g
> Protein: ?

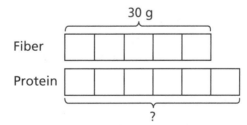

> There are 5 units of fiber and 6 units of protein.

5 units = 30 g
1 unit = 30 g ÷ 5 = 6 g
6 units = 6 g × 6 = 36 g

The cereal bar contains 36 grams of protein.

notes

📰 Problem 2 – *Sports Club Problem*

The ratio of boys to girls in a sports club is 5 : 3. There are 30 more boys than girls. How many children are there in the sports club?

First, get a sense of the data. Then, draw a bar model to represent this data.

I can represent the ratio 5 : 3 using a bar model.

Boy

Girl

Now, transfer the data from the word problem into the model.

In this problem, the quantity for the difference is given. There are 30 more boys than girls.

Boy

Girl

?

30

There are 8 units of children altogether in the sports club.

2 units = 30
1 unit = 30 ÷ 2 = 15
8 units = 8 × 15 = 120

There are 120 children in the sports club.

Learning Point

For ratio problems similar to the ones we have just seen, we can use a comparison model to represent the quantities in the problem. The quantities given are either for the parts, the whole or the difference. A bar model shows the relationship between the quantities visually and helps students decide on the mathematical procedure to use. We can solve the problem once we have established the number of units representing the given quantities.

Practice 1

Solve these word problems by drawing appropriate bar models. Detailed solutions can be found at the end of this chapter.

1. The lengths of the sides of a triangle are in the ratio 3 : 4 : 5. If the perimeter of the triangle is 180 cm, what is the length of the longest side?

 75 cm

2. Fertilizer and water were mixed in the ratio 1 : 4. If 15 litres more water than fertilizer was used in the mixture, how much fertilizer was used?

 5 L

Chapter 4: *Ratio*

Let us look at some other problems involving ratio.

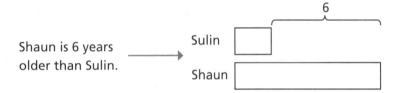

Problem 3 – *Age Problem*

Shaun is 6 years older than Sulin. In 3 years' time, the ratio of Sulin's age to Shaun's age will be 2 : 5. How old is Sulin now?

First, get a sense of the data. Then, draw a bar model to represent this data.

Shaun is 6 years older than Sulin. ⟶

```
                          6
                    ⌐‾‾‾‾‾‾‾‾‾¬
Sulin   [        ]
Shaun   [                        ]
```

> The model above does not help me solve the problem as I do not know the number of units representing the given quantity.

> I will draw a model to show the ratio of their ages in 3 years' time instead.

In 3 year's time:

Sulin : Shaun
  2 : 5   ⟶

```
Sulin   [    |    ]
Shaun   [    |    |    |    |    ]
```

> What quantity do I know? How can I use this model to solve the problem?

The difference in their ages in 3 years' time will be unchanged!

Shaun will always be 6 years older than Sulin. So, I mark the difference in their ages on the bar model.

6

Sulin

Shaun

3 units = 6
1 unit = 6 ÷ 3 = 2
2 units = 2 × 2 = 4

Sulin will be 4 years old in 3 years' time.

4 – 3 = 1

So, Sulin is 1 year old now.

notes

Problem 4 – *Eggs Problem*

notes

The ratio of the number of chicken eggs to the number of duck eggs Farmer Lee had on Monday was 3 : 4. While putting the eggs into a carton, Farmer Lee broke 12 chicken eggs and the ratio of the number of chicken eggs to the number of duck eggs became 1 : 2. How many chicken eggs did Farmer Lee have at first?

First, get a sense of the data. Then, draw a bar model to represent this data.

Before:

At first, the ratio was 3 : 4.

Chicken eggs

Duck eggs

After:

The ratio became 1 : 2.

Chicken eggs

Duck eggs

Since the number of duck eggs remained the same, I can make the number of units representing the duck eggs the same as the earlier one, that is, 4.

Since 1 : 2 = 2 : 4, we get:

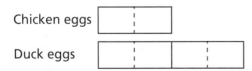

Chicken eggs

Duck eggs

Chapter 4: *Ratio*

We know that the number of duck eggs remained the same and the number of chicken eggs reduced by 12. So, we compare the chicken eggs using 'before' and 'after' models.

Before:

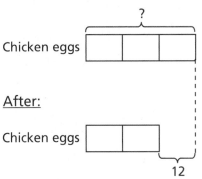

Chicken eggs

After:

Chicken eggs

1 unit = 12
3 units = 12 × 3 = 36

Farmer Lee had 36 chicken eggs at first.

 **Learning Point**

For some ratio problems, it is useful to identify quantities which remain unchanged and solve the problem based on this information. For example, in Problem 3, the difference in the ages between the two people is a constant. We can use this constant as the given quantity and equate it to the difference in units reflected in the age ratio to help us solve the problem. In Problem 4, we identify the quantity that is constant and manipulate the ratio to reflect the constant.

Chapter 4: *Ratio*

Practice 2

Solve these word problems by drawing appropriate bar models. Detailed solutions can be found at the end of this chapter.

1. Grace is 4 years old when John is 7 years old. In how many years' time will the ratio of Grace's age to John's age be 4 : 5?

 8

2. The ratio of the number of adults to the number of children at a party was 12 : 7. After 78 children left, the ratio of the number of adults to the number of children became 3 : 1. How many children were there at the party at first?

182

Chapter 4: *Ratio*

Reflections

- We can use fractions and ratios interchangeably as both can be represented using bar models.

- For word problems involving ratio, we can either

  (a) assign the given quantity to the number of units representing the parts, whole or difference shown in the bar model, or

  (b) identify the quantity that remains unchanged and manipulate the ratio around that thinking.

How can you apply what you have learned in this chapter to provide your students with a more visual approach to understanding ratio and developing proportional reasoning skills?

Try This...

- Create a word problem involving ratio that your students generally have difficulties with.

- Use the Bar Model Method to solve the problem you created. Highlight the critical teaching points in the solution.

Solutions

Practice 1

1.

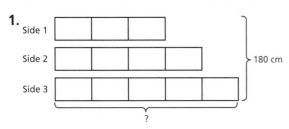

3 + 4 + 5 = 12
12 units = 180 cm
1 unit = 180 cm ÷ 12 = 15 cm
5 units = 15 cm × 5 = 75 cm

The longest side of the triangle is 75 cm.

2.

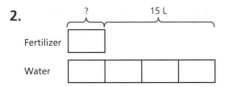

3 units = 15 L
1 unit = 15 L ÷ 3 = 5 L

5 litres of fertilizer was used.

Practice 2

1. Difference in ages = 7 − 4 = 3

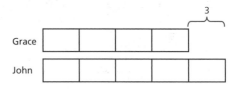

1 unit = 3
4 units = 3 × 4 = 12 (Grace's age)
12 − 4 = 8

In 8 years' time, the ratio of Grace's age to John's age will be 4 : 5.

2. Before:

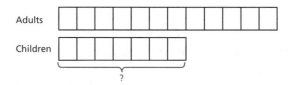

After:

78 children left the party. No change to the length of the bar model representing adults. The number of adults is now represented by 3 units. New ratio — 3 : 1.

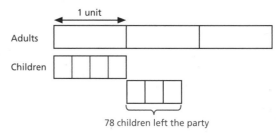

78 children left the party

3 units = 78
1 unit = 78 ÷ 3 = 26
7 units = 26 × 7 = 182

There were 182 children at the party at first.

notes

Percentage

Word problems involving the part-whole model

We can use a bar model to represent fractions, ratio and also percentage.

Look at the figure below.

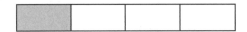

We can describe the shaded part in the figure in these three ways:

1. Since 1 out of the 4 equal parts is shaded, we can say that $\frac{1}{4}$ of the figure is shaded.

2. The ratio of the shaded part to the whole figure is 1 : 4.

3. 25% of the figure is shaded.

Let us look more closely at how we derive the percentage in the third statement.

Consider this: If we divide a whole into 100 equal units, each unit is $\frac{1}{100}$ or 1% of the whole:

$\frac{1}{100}$ or 1% of the whole

100 equal units

Now, look at the earlier figure again.

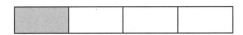

If we divide this figure into 100 equal units, we have:

$$\frac{1}{4} = \frac{25}{100} = 25\%$$

This can also be illustrated as a bar model in the following way:

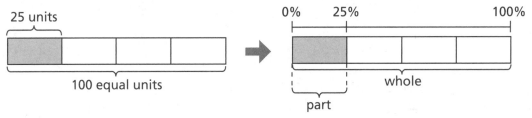

25% of the whole is shaded

The whole is taken as the base, which is 100%. We can think of this 100% as 100 units.

So, if the whole has a quantity of 200, then 25% of the whole can be worked out as:

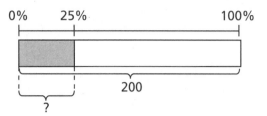

100 units = 200
1 unit = 200 ÷ 100 = 2
25 units = 2 × 25 = 50

So 25% of 200 is 50.

Let us look at a word problem involving percentage and how we can use a part-whole model to help us visualize and solve the problem.

📋 Problem 1 – *Exhibition Problem*

There were 160 adults and some children at an exhibition. 80% of the people at the exhibition were adults. How many children were there?

First, get a sense of the data. Then, draw a model to represent this data.

I know the whole (adults and children) is 100%. I am also given the percentage for the adults.

I first draw a bar to represent the whole, which is 100%.

0%   100%

notes

I can think of 100% as 100 units. So, 80% is 80 units. I estimate and mark 80% of the whole to represent the adults. The remaining part will represent the children.

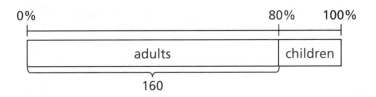

$100\% - 80\% = 20\%$

So, the number of children is represented by 20% of the whole, or 20 units.

80 units = 160
1 unit = 160 ÷ 80 = 2
20 units = 20 × 2 = 40

There were 40 children.

Alternatively, we can work out the answer using percentages(%) instead of units:

80% represents 160   80% → 160
1% represents ...   1% → 160 ÷ 80 = 2
20% represents ...   20% → 20 × 2 = 40

For this method, I use arrows instead of '=' to indicate 'represents' because the percentage is not equivalent to the quantity. For example: $80\% = 0.8 \neq 160$

🎯 Learning Point

The whole or the base which the given percentage in the problem refers to is taken as 100%. Drawing a bar model will enable students to visualize this 100% as 100 units. By equating the quantity given in the problem to the number of units, students will be able to solve the problem easily.

Practice 1

Solve these word problems by drawing appropriate bar models. Detailed solutions can be found at the end of this chapter.

1. James sorted out his collection of game cards and found that 40% of his game cards were torn. If he had 350 games cards altogether, how many game cards were torn?

 140

2. There were 25 000 people at the stadium watching a soccer match. Among them, 52% were men, 20% were children and the rest were women. How many women were there at the stadium?

 7000

3. A survey found that 12% of the students in a particular school travel to school by car, 62% travel by bus while the rest walk. If 84 students travel to school by car, how many students walk to school?

 182

4. Every month, Sam spends 65% of his salary on rent and 15% on food. He saves the rest. He saves $130 more than what he spends on food. What is his monthly salary?

 $2600

Word problems involving the comparison model

When we compare two or more quantities using percentages, we draw a comparison model to help us visualize the quantities. For the two bars drawn, we need to be clear which quantity is taken as the base (100%).

For example, if we say 'A is 80% of B', we take B as the base.
In this case, B is 100% and A is 80%. We draw the bar model in this way:

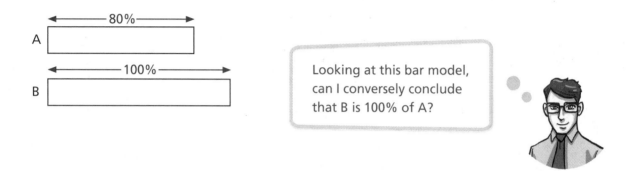

Looking at this bar model, can I conversely conclude that B is 100% of A?

No, that statement would not be correct. The model above shows the percentage of A with respect to B (the base), not the percentage of B with respect to A. Percentage is used relative to another quantity which is the base (or 100%). By drawing the appropriate bar model, students will be visually aware of which quantity the base is.

Given the above scenario where 'A is 80% of B', there is also a tendency for students to make the following statements:

1. A is 20% less than B
2. B is 20% more than A

Without the bar model, it may be difficult to explain to students why the first statement is correct while the second statement is not.

For the statement 'A is 20% less than B', we are finding the percentage of A with respect to B. So, we take B as the base. This corresponds to the bar model above where B is shown to be 100%. As A is 80% on the bar model, it is correct to say that 'A is 20% less than B'.

To say that 'B is 20% more than A', we are finding the percentage of B with respect to A. So, we should take A as the base.

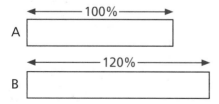

We shall deal with this in the next two problems presented in this chapter.

Problem 2 – *Stickers Problem*

Meena has 56 stickers. She has 80% as many stickers as Nelly. What percentage of Meena's stickers does Nelly have?

First, get a sense of the data. Then, draw a bar model to represent this data.

Meena has 80% as many stickers as Nelly. So Nelly has more stickers than Meena.

The given percentage compares Meena's stickers to Nelly's stickers. So, we take Nelly's stickers as the base (100%).

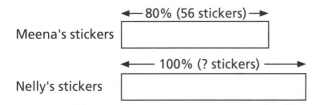

Meena's stickers ⟵ 80% (56 stickers) ⟶

Nelly's stickers ⟵ 100% (? stickers) ⟶

Can I say that Nelly has 20% more stickers than Meena? This would mean that Nelly has 120% as many stickers as Meena.

Lee us see if this is true.

$$80\% \rightarrow 56$$
$$1\% \rightarrow 56 \div 80 = 0.7$$
$$100\% \rightarrow 0.7 \times 100 = 70$$

So, Nelly has 70 stickers.

To find Nelly's stickers as a percentage of Meena's stickers, we now take Meena's stickers as the base (100%).

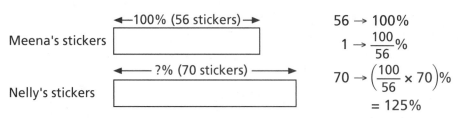

Meena's stickers $\longleftarrow$ 100% (56 stickers) $\longrightarrow$

Nelly's stickers $\longleftarrow$?% (70 stickers) $\longrightarrow$

$56 \rightarrow 100\%$

$1 \rightarrow \dfrac{100}{56}\%$

$70 \rightarrow \left(\dfrac{100}{56} \times 70\right)\%$

$= 125\%$

Nelly has 125% of Meena's stickers (and not 120%!).

 Problem 3 – *Money Problem*

Alan says "I have 20% less money than you, Ben." Ben says "That means I have 20% more money than you, Alan." If we know that Ben has $160 and Alan is correct, is Ben's statement also correct?

First, get a sense of the data. Then, draw a bar model to represent this data.

I know that Alan has 20% less money than Ben. I shall draw a model using Ben's amount as the base and find out first how much money Alan has.

We take Ben's amount to be the base. So, Ben's amount is taken as 100%. Since Alan has 20% less money than Ben, Alan's amount is 80%.

Ben's amount $\longleftarrow$ 100% ($160) $\longrightarrow$

Alan's amount $\longleftarrow$ 80% ($?) $\longrightarrow$

$100\% \rightarrow \$160$

$1\% \rightarrow \$\dfrac{160}{100}$

$80\% \rightarrow \$\left(\dfrac{160}{100} \times 80\right)$

$= \$128$

Alan has $128.

So, if Ben has $160, then Alan has $128.

Now that we know the amounts of money they both have, let us see if Ben's statement is correct.

$160 − $128 = $32

Ben has $32 more than Alan.

Chapter 5: Percentage

To express this difference ($32) as a percentage of Alan's amount, we now take Alan's amount as the base.

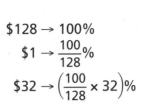

Ben's amount
← ($160) →

Alan's amount
← 100% ($128) →
?% ($32)

$128 → 100%

$1 → $\frac{100}{128}$%

$32 → $\left(\frac{100}{128} \times 32\right)$%

= 25%

Ben has 25% more than Alan (and not 20%!).

So, Ben's statement that he has 20% more than Alan is incorrect.

 Learning Point

When we compare quantities using percentage, it is important to know that the quantity to which it is compared should be taken as 100%.

For example,

If we say that A is 80% as much as B, or A is 20% less than B, we take B to be the base(100%).

A
← 80% →

B
← 100% →

If we wish to compare B with A, then we need to consider A to be the base.
Taking A to be the base now, we have:

A
← 80 units (100%) →

B
← 100 units (?%) →

80 units → 100%

1 unit → $\frac{100}{80}$%

100 units → $\left(\frac{100}{80} \times 100\right)$%

= 125%

So, B is 125% of A, or B is 25% more than A.

Practice 2

Solve these word problems by drawing appropriate bar models. Detailed solutions can be found at the end of this chapter.

1. Shane has $70. Lee has 10% more money than Shane. How much money does Lee have?

 $77

2. Jose's salary is $2500. Peter earns 60% as much as Jose. What percentage of Peter's salary is Jose's salary?

 $166\frac{2}{3}\%$

Chapter 5: *Percentage*

3. Box A has a mass of 10 kg. Box B is 20% lighter than Box A. How many percent heavier is Box A than Box B?

 25%

Reflections

- When solving word problems involving percentage, we must determine which quantity the base is. The base must always be taken as 100% or 100 units.

- For word problems which compare two quantities, the quantity which is compared to should be taken as 100%.

- Note that if A is *x*% more than B, that does not imply that B is *x*% less than A.

How can you use the Bar Model Method to help your students relate their understanding of whole numbers, fractions and ratio to percentage?

Try This...

- Create a word problem involving percentage that your students generally have difficulties with. Consider how working through this problem reinforces the concept of percentage.

- Use the Bar Model Method to solve the problem you created. Highlight the critical teaching points in the solution.

Solutions

Practice 1

1.

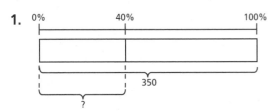

100% → 350
1% → 350 ÷ 100 = 3.5
40% → 3.5 × 40 = 140

140 game cards were torn.

2.

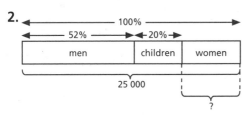

100% − 52% − 20% = 28%
100% → 25 000
1% → 25 000 ÷ 100 = 250
28% → 28 × 250 = 7000

There were 7000 women at the stadium.

3.

12% → 84
1% → 84 ÷ 12 = 7
100% − 12% − 62% = 26%
26% → 26 × 7 = 182

182 students walk to school.

4.

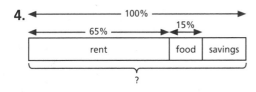

100% − 65% − 15% = 20%

He saves 20%.

20% − 15% = 5%
5% → $130
1% → $130 ÷ 5 = $26
100% → $26 × 100 = $2600

His monthly salary is $2600.

Practice 2

1.

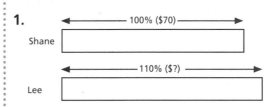

100% → $70
1% → $$\frac{70}{100} = \$\frac{7}{10}$$
110% → $$\$\frac{7}{10} \times 110 = \$77$$

Lee has $77.

2.

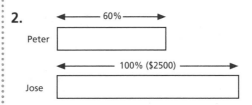

100% → $2500
1% → $2500 ÷ 100 = $25
60% → $25 × 60 = $1500

So, Peter earns $1500.

$$\frac{2500}{1500} \times 100\% = 166\frac{2}{3}\%$$

Jose's salary is $166\frac{2}{3}\%$ of Peter's salary.

3.

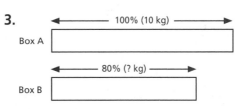

80% of 10 kg = 8 kg
10 kg − 8 kg = 2 kg

Box A is 2 kg heavier than Box B.

$$\frac{2}{8} \times 100\% = 25\%$$

Box A is 25% heavier than Box B.

notes

✎ notes

REFERENCES

Bruner, J. S. (1961). The act of discovery. *Harvard Educational Review, 31*, pp. 21–32.

Greeno, J. G. (1978). A study of problem solving. In R. Glaser (Ed.), *Advances in instructional psychology* (Vol. 1), pp.13–75. Hillsdale, NJ: Lawrence Erlbaum Associates.

Kho, T.H., Yeo, S. M., & Lim, J. (2009). *The Singapore Model Method for Learning Mathematics.* Singapore: EPB Pan Pacific.

Nesher, P., Greeno, J. G., & Riley, M.S. (1982). The development of semantic categories for addition and subtraction. *Educational Studies in Mathematics, 13,* pp. 373–394.

Polya, G. (1945). How to Solve It. Princeton, NJ: Princeton University Press.

TIMSS & PIRLS International Study Center. *TIMSS International Results in Mathematics.* Retrieved from http://www.timss.org

Further readings:

Fuson, K.C. (1992). Research on whole number addition and subtraction. In D.A. Grouws (Ed.) *Handbook of Research on Mathematics Teaching and Learning*, pp. 243–275. New York: Macmillan.

Kho, T.H. (1987). Mathematical models for solving arithmetic problems. *Proceedings of the Fourth Southeast Asian Conference on Mathematical Education (ICMI-SEAMS). Mathematical Education in the 1990's,* pp. 345–351. Singapore: Institute of Education.

Singapore Ministry of Education. (2013). *Primary Mathematics Teaching and Learning Syllabus.* Curriculum Planning and Development Division, Ministry of Education, Singapore. Retrieved from http://www.moe.gov. sg/education/syllabuses/sciences/files/ maths-primary-2013. pdf

Nesher, P. (1992). Solving multiplication word problems. In G. Leinhardt, R. T. Putnam, & R. Hattrup (Eds.), *Analysis of Arithmetic for Mathematics Teaching,* pp. 189–220. Hillsdale, NJ: Lawrence Erlbaum Associates.

Ng, S.F., & Lee, K. (2009). The Model Method: Singapore children's tool for representing and solving algebraic word problems. *Journal for Research in Mathematics Education*, 40(3), pp. 282–313.

Smith, J. P. (2002). The development of students' knowledge of fractions and ratios. In B. Litwiller & G. Bright (Eds.), *Making Sense of Fractions, Ratios and Proportions: 2002 Yearbook*, pp. 3–17. Reston, VA: National Council of Teachers of Mathematics.

Also available in the **PR1ME**™ series:

SCHOLASTIC
PR1ME™
Mathematics
Proven to be world's best practice

Scholastic **PR1ME**™ Mathematics is a world class program
constructed on a composite of standards and effective
teaching and learning practices of the global top-performers
in Mathematics — Singapore, Republic of Korea and Hong Kong,
in collaboration with Ministry of Education in Singapore.

Use world's best practice to teach Mathematics

Globally, the three nations that have topped Trends in International Mathematics and Science Study (TIMSS) are Singapore, Republic of Korea and Hong Kong. **Scholastic PR1ME**™ **Mathematics** combines the best practice pedagogy from these three nations and has been adapted from the highly acclaimed and widely proven Primary Mathematics Project developed by the Ministry of Education in Singapore. The result is a comprehensive and proven mathematics approach that works!

Available for Grades 1–6:
Coursebooks, Practice Books, Teacher's Guides and Interactive Whiteboard component

Why **PR1ME**™ Mathematics works

1. Explicit problem solving is at the center for teaching and learning — with an emphasis on both the processes and strategies, including the bar model
2. Students learn through consistent pedagogy and a concrete-pictorial-abstract approach
3. Topics take a 'deep dive' into the development of concepts to build mastery through scaffolding
4. Students actively develop metalanguage and metacognitive thinking
5. Teachers' professional learning is enhanced through using world's best practice